AROUND
NEWARK
IN OLD PHOTOGRAPHS

A PASTORAL VIEW OF NEWARK, c. 1910, showing some principal landmarks: the castle, parish church of St Mary, corn exchange and wooden 'haleing' bridge. The latter, built in c. 1827, carried the Trent Navigation towpath over the Mill Race (from where this picture was taken). Both bridge and the Swan and Salmon Inn behind are no longer extant.

Front Cover Illustration:
PERHAPS THE MOST EVOCATIVE VIEW OF NEWARK. The spire and west entrance to the parish church of St Mary from Kirkgate, seen here in c. 1920.

AROUND
NEWARK
IN OLD PHOTOGRAPHS

_____COMPILED BY_____
TIM WARNER

ALAN SUTTON
Published in collaboration with

**Nottinghamshire County Council
Leisure Services**

Alan Sutton Publishing
Phoenix Mill · Far Thrupp · Stroud · Gloucestershire

First published 1991

British Library Cataloguing in Publication Data

Around Newark in old photographs.
I. Warner, Tim, *1962–*
942.2524

ISBN 0-86299-890-5

Typeset in 9/10 Korinna.
Typesetting and orgination by
Alan Sutton Publishing Limited.
Printed in Great Britain by
The Bath Press, Avon.

CONTENTS

INTRODUCTION   6

1.   INTRODUCING NEWARK   9

2.   SCHOOLDAYS   21

3.   WORK   31

4.   RECREATION   49

5.   SHOPPING   71

6.   MEMORABLE EVENTS   85

7.   AROUND NEWARK   103

     ACKNOWLEDGEMENTS   160

'Fear of the present leads to a mystification of the past ...'
John Berger, *Ways of Seeing*, 1972

INTRODUCTION

'The old world was well-nigh exhausted. . . . Then
all at once breaks a small light in the far west,
and a new world slowly widens to our sight – new
sky, new earth, new flowers, a very heaven compared
with the old earth. . . .'

Writing in 1848, these were the thoughts of the well known Victorian sculptor and
Royal Academician, Joseph Durham (1814–1877), upon first witnessing the
results of the new science of photography.

In today's world of 'instant' full colour 'snaps' it is hard to appreciate the
wonderment – incredulity almost – that Durham and his contemporaries felt when
confronted with the new medium. So inured are we to photographic images, and
so dim with age are many nineteenth-century photographs, that it is impossible to
realise how bright, how clear, how *new* they originally appeared to Victorian eyes.
Of course the element of colour was missing, but what it lacked in colour
photography made up for by a miraculous double measure of precision.

Precision, however, was not to everyone's taste. Many artists, for instance,
considered the sheer speed and clarity of the new process incapable of producing
true works of art. As painting's poor relation, photographs were seen as devoid of
feeling and lacking the moral virtues of labour and study. In practical terms,
however, the machinations of remote aesthetes were of little relevance. The
eminent practicality and economy of photography meant that its success as a
means of mass communication was never seriously in doubt. In the wake of its rise
to supremacy many hitherto popular methods of illustration, notably lithography
and engraving, were to disappear almost entirely.

To all intents and purposes the invention of photography may be attributed to
Louis Daguerre and William Henry Fox Talbot. Working independently in France
and England they had, by 1841, all but perfected the chemical processes that still
underpin photography as we know it today. With their discovery came the rapid
growth of photography as a commercial enterprise, a situation graphically revealed
in Britain through the national census returns. In 1861 2,534 individuals registered
themselves as professional photographers; by 1901 the figure had risen to in
excess of 17,000. This trend is mirrored (albeit tardily and in miniature) in Newark.

The first reference to a photographer in the town appears in the trade directory
of 1864 when James Oman of Appletongate advertised his services as 'Artist
Photographer'. By 1869 Oman had been joined by Samuel Frost of 6 Kirkgate and
John McLeod whose studio address is given as Trent Bridge. Between 1869 and

1897 the number of professional photographers registered in Newark remained constant at three, the town apparently being unable to support any more. Nevertheless, in January of that year (1897) the *Newark Advertiser* announced the formation of the town's first Camera Club charged with encouraging and promoting photography as a suitable hobby among local amateurs.

The Newark Camera Club was formed at a time when photography was experiencing a national boom in popularity, due in no small measure to the appearance in 1888 of Kodak's first 'push-button' camera. Claiming a simplicity hitherto unheard of, their advertising slogan confidently proclaimed 'Everyone can use it: everyone *will* use it'.

In spite of such claims, however, true push-botton photography was still many years hence. Exposure times were still measured in tens rather than hundredths of seconds, and stiff studio portraits – made stiffer by neck clamps – were the norm. The inability of cameras to capture the rapidity of everyday life means there are many fewer early photographs of ordinary people doing ordinary things than today's social historians would like. It was not really until the end of Victoria's reign that technology began to allow the candid 'snapshot' to convey the spontaneity of life as it was lived.

Nevertheless, despite these limitations, such subjects proved an increasingly irresistable lure to photographers in towns like Newark. And it is to this socio-historic record of town life that the present volume is largely devoted. Although the 'standard' carte-de-visite or postcard views of Newark and its environs are represented, the bulk of the collection draws on a wealth of privately owned photographs loaned by residents of the town and published here for the first time.

Although few of the photographers who took these pictures left extensive biographical details, in one instance at least we are fortunate. Of central import-ance to the production of this book has been the work of Mr N.J. Antoine, and the following biographical information was provided by his widow and daughter who still live in the town.

The Antoines came to Newark just before the outbreak of the Second World War in 1939. Mr Antoine worked at Hunt's photographic studio in Cawkwell's Yard off Stodman Street. At that time the studio specialized mainly in formal portraits of local dignitaries or family groups, occasionally contributing shots to the local newspapers, the *Newark Advertiser* and *Newark Herald*. After the war, in 1947, Mr Antoine opened his own photographic business at nos. 26–28 Cartergate, ultimately taking over Hunt's business. What is most important for us, however, is that on top of his formal photographic work at the studio, Mr Antoine spent much of his spare time photographing everyday life on the streets of Newark. The results of his endeavours, scattered liberally throughout this book, present an unpar-ralleled record of Newark in the 1940s and '50s.

So, what can we say of the Newark in times past as revealed by the work of Mr Antoine and his compatriots? Firstly, it is suggested, in topography at least, the life-long Newarker will find remarkably little has changed in the fabric of the town. Despite containing buildings dating back to the twelfth century, the characteristic architecture of Newark is decidedly late eighteenth/early nineteenth century, the former being illustrated most eloquently by the classical Town Hall. Views of the town and its buildings are covered by Section 1, 'Introducing Newark'.

Section 2, 'Schooldays', concentrates, as its title suggests, on pictures of school life over the last 100 years or so. Foremost among the photographs here are a remarkable series from the Thomas Magnus School depicting pupils, both formally and informally, prior to the school's removal from Appletongate to Earp Avenue. Whereas formal class portraits from all Newark's schools are plentiful, such delightfully candid shots of boarders and day-boys present a unique record of an educational system long gone.

Research for Section 3, 'Work', revealed that pictures of people doing their everyday jobs were especially rare. This is, perhaps, not surprising when one considers that even today few people would consider their own jobs interesting enough to warrant photographing. Nevertheless, one or two notable exceptions did come to light. Photographs supplied by British Gypsum Ltd (pp 31–2) provide a graphic impression of work at their Hawton quarry, while pictures of Mr Ernest Parnham in Quibell's laboratory and the Newark 'night soil' collectors (both p 47) give a vivid insight into areas of work long removed from the town.

In contrast, by far the most prolific fund of pictures available came under the heading 'Recreation' (Section 4). Here are presented many of the leisure activities that, over the years, have excited and amused the residents of Newark. The range is truly diverse, and the section ends with a series of pictures tracing the once annual and much supported 'Sunday School Treat'.

Section 5, 'Shopping', makes extensive use of the Antoine Collection which records many well remembered shop frontages from the 1940s and '50s. Sprinkled among these are more intimate views of individual shops and their keepers supplied by relatives from their private albums.

The final section on Newark (Section 6, 'Memorable Events'), presents extracts from what might be termed the civic history of the town: royal visits, coronations, gala performances and visiting celebrities are all represented along with events which are memorable for less joyous reasons: disasters such as fires and floods.

The book ends with a look at some of the villages 'Around Newark' from which the town draws much of its trade and, indeed, character. By contrast with the predominantly industrial nature of Newark, life as photographed in the villages reveals a broad agricultural base which then, as now, underpins the urban economy of Newark.

Photographs of Newark's fine and historic buildings abound, and could easily fill a book in their own right. This compilation, however, concentrates on the people of Newark, for it is people who determine the character and fortunes of a place. Equally, without the assistance and generosity of the people of Newark, it would not have been possible to produce this volume. In addition to those many individuals – too numerous to mention by name – who supplied invaluable background information, I extend my sincere thanks to all those whose pictures make up this glimpse at Newark past.

Tim Warner,
Newark,
August 1991

Introducing Newark

BEASTMARKET HILL, C. 1900. The Ossington Coffee Palace (left) was built in 1882 by Viscountess Ossington as a temperance hotel. Situated opposite the cattle market it was intended to lure farmers away from the town pubs. It was never very successful. The eighteenth-century town house beneath the church was the home of the Warwick brewing family.

CASTLEGATE, 1942. Here, Warwick's house is occupied by Castle Motors which took over the premises in the mid-1920s. They remained until 1972 when Holdens furniture shop moved in. Behind the 'bus at no. 5 is the shop of George Lineker (watchmaker) who retained the honour of winding the church clock.

WILLIAM GILSTRAP (of Gilstrap, Earp & Co., maltsters) viewing the newly completed Gilstrap Free Library – his gift to the town – prior to its official opening in July 1883. Costing £10,000, it was designed by William Henman of Birmingham. Behind, in the castle grounds, stood the cattle market which had been moved from Beastmarket Hill in 1839.

THE CATTLE MARKET was removed from the castle in 1886 and the grounds were laid out as pleasure gardens. 'Nobly done Newark!' proclaimed the *Newark Advertiser* at their opening in May 1889. The layout of flower beds (partially seen here) resembled the letters V.O.O.C. Locals were quick to interpret the apparent acronym as 'Very Old Old Castle'.

THE POPULARITY OF THE PLEASURE GROUNDS led to further gardens across the Trent. The New Castle Gardens (far right) were opened by the Duchess of Newcastle in July 1912. She praised the excellence of their design, while Alderman Knight saw the delightful July weather as 'a happy augury for the success of the new grounds'.

LUNY PARK, NEWARK. *Aug. 29th, 1912.*

THE GARDENS WERE COMPLETELY FLOODED only a month later, and the whole venture derisively re-named 'Luny Park' by the townsfolk. Alderman Knight couldn't have been more wrong. In fairness, however, the possibility of *winter* flooding had been foreseen, but that it should happen in high summer stirred this photographer to frame his picture with a sharp sense of irony.

THE LONGSTONE BRIDGE carries the Trent Navigation towpath over the weir at Newark to this day. The tall building behind is the Trent Brewery, opened by Messrs Richardson, Earp & Slater in 1857. In 1889 the Trent Brewery Co. amalgamated with Richard Warwick & Sons Ltd. To the left of the brewery is the tannery.

MARKET PLACE, 1930s. When not in use the market stalls used to be cleared away. Shops in this view include Currys cycles, Stennets printers and publishers of the *Newark Herald* (ceased 1960), J.H. Phillips rope manufacturers, Coynes musical instruments and G.H. Porter grocers. Dominating all is the majestic spire of the twelfth-century church of St Mary.

BRIDGE STREET, C. 1930. Along the north (right) side Dewhurst the butchers, the Maypole Dairy and J. Mills & Son boot and shoe dealers may be seen. On the south (left) side are J.H. Smith chemists and Freeman Hardy Willis Ltd, bootmakers.

NEWARK'S MAIN POST OFFICE between 1889 and 1908 was at no. 15 Cartergate (now Whistler's chemist). This picture, taken in 1904, shows some of the services then available, including parcel post, savings bank and telegraph. A more recently installed sign advertises the arrival of the telephone.

THE NEW, PURPOSE-BUILT POST OFFICE IN KIRKGATE. Business was transferred here from Cartergate in February 1908. Designed by Saunders & Saunders (architects) of Newark, and built by George Brown & Son, the main façade was described by the *Newark Advertiser* as 'a poem in stone'. The first postmaster here was Mr N.W. Bolton.

PANORAMA OF NEWARK from Hole's Albert Street (Castle) brewery, 1930, the horizon blurred by smoke from the industrial sector. Bottom left is the old 'bus station with open-top gents' toilets. When double-deckers were introduced after the Second World War the toilets had to be closed as top deck passengers could see in.

BEAUMOND CROSS in 1907 in its original position at the junction of Cartergate, Lombard Street and Albert Street. Dating from the fourteenth century, the cross has now been safely relocated in Beaumond Gardens where its antiquity contrasts starkly with the town's new award-winning glass library.

ONE OF NEWARK'S VANISHED SPLENDOURS: the Chauntry House was demolished in 1919 to make way for the Palace Theatre. One of the country's finest Queen Anne-style buildings, the Chauntry House was built in 1702–14 by Samuel Foster, although it is best remembered as the residence of three-times mayor of Newark, Joseph Sikes.

THE CHAUNTRY HOUSE, as the name suggests, was built on the site of a chauntry or residence for priests serving the chauntries of the church. As a private residence it maintained its own chapel (pictured here). Upon demolition the tower and clock were incorporated into the Magnus School buildings on Earp Avenue.

COTTAGES IN KIRKGATE, 1937. In the doorway half-way down at no. 6 are Miss Elizabeth Cobb and her nephew, Arthur Mathews. They are at the entrance to Miss Cobb's shop which she lived above. These cottages have now been demolished and their place taken by a second-hand car sales business.

DEMOLITION OF 'GEORGE III' COTTAGES in Hardy's Yard behind the Governor's House, 1930. Hunt & Co.'s photographic studio (from where many of the pictures in this book originate via Mr N.J. Antoine who worked there) was situated on the left hand side of the yard.

'RAILWAY CARRIAGE HOUSE', Lincoln Road. A national housing shortage in the 1920s led to a move toward self-build. At first many started with inexpensive materials such as redundant railway carriages or even tents. As finances allowed, refinements could be added. Here, Mr Hopkinson, the owner (on motorbike), already has a verandah, tiled roof and chimney.

BARNBYGATE METHODIST CHAPEL was opened on 2 July 1846 after former premises on Guildhall Street proved insufficient. The architect was James Simpson and the building cost £5,261 18s. 4d. To the right stands the Bedehouse, its almshouses and chapel. Built with money from the Phillipot charity, all but the chapel were demolished in the 1950s.

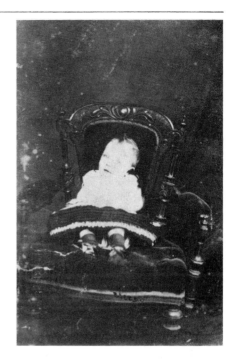

ONE OF THE NEWEST INHABITANTS of Jubilee Street, William Riley, who was born into one of the houses recently completed and named in commemoration of Queen Victoria's Golden Jubilee in 1887.

SALVATIONISTS (right, back) from Newark Salvation Army with the children of Water Lane, 1890s. One of the poorest and most run-down areas of the town, most of the buildings in Water Lane were demolished in 1905.

JAMES AND MARY SMITH of Water Lane, Newark, c. 1861. They were married at Christmas 1852 and Mr Smith worked as a maltster at James Hole & Co.'s brewery. Their home in Water Lane lay in one of the poorest (and roughest) areas of the town.

LUCY SMITH, daughter of James and Mary Smith of Water Lane. Photographed in c. 1861.

SECTION TWO

Schooldays

LIFE IN NEWARK'S JERSEY SCHOOL (founded 1623) on Guildhall Street centred around the production of jersey (worsted) stockings. Over 1,000 pairs were made annually. Among the pupils here (c. 1890) are Clara Boyes, Sally Lawson, Gwen Jex and Gertie Hickerby, together with Headmistress Miss Morley. The school closed in 1901.

NEWARK'S SCIENCE AND ART SCHOOL was built entirely by public subscription at a cost of £3,154 as a memorial to Queen Victoria's Diamond Jubilee in 1897. The upper storey was devoted to art teaching (where large windows afforded excellent light), while science was confined to the ground floor.

STAFF AND PUPILS AT THE SCIENCE AND ART SCHOOL on London Road, c. 1900. The Principal (front, centre) was the Revd Andrew Ping. In 1910 the building became home to the new Lilley & Stone School, successor to the Jersey School which had hitherto been beneficiary of the Lilley & Stone charity.

A CLASSROOM AT THE LILLEY & STONE SCHOOL in c. 1915. The teacher is thought to be Miss M.M. Skues (headmistress 1906–16). Girls were required to take an entrance exam (at age 10) and, in 1939, tuition fees were £4 4s. per term.

NEWARK TECHNICAL COLLEGE, 1931. When the Lilley & Stone School moved to London Road, space for the Science and Art School became severely limited. In 1920, however, they were able to purchase Chauntry Park and build new premises, which were re-named Newark Technical College and opened in 1931 at a cost of £25,000.

THE GRAMMAR SCHOOL in Newark was originally endowed by Thomas Magnus (Archbishop of Yorkshire's West Riding) in 1532. A new site was obtained on Appletongate and the school prospered. In the 1850s further buildings were added (pictured here) largely obscuring Magnus' original 'Tudor Hall'. In 1909 the school moved again to its present site on Earp Avenue.

A GROUP OF MAGNUS BOARDERS in their best uniforms, 1890s. Boarders appear to have been first taken alongside day boys in c. 1820. Boarding ceased in 1932. The small boy (front right) is *not* a boarder. He is Cyril Noakes, son of E. Spencer Noakes, headmaster from 1894 to 1904.

BARE WALLS AND NAKED GAS MANTELS were the backdrop to classes at the Magnus in the 1890s. Education was predominantly classical, intended to prepare the boys for Oxbridge. Day boys paid nothing for tuition in 'core' subjects (the 3 Rs), but a fee was charged for extras such as History or Geography.

LIFE AT THE MAGNUS WAS NOT ALL STUDY. Conkers was a favourite, as was Fives, with specially constructed courts which are pictured here in the playground at Appletongate. Bearing some similarity to squash, in Fives the ball is hit with a gloved hand. If ungloved, the hand swelled impressively.

MAGNUS CRICKET TEAM, C. 1863. Distinctive scarlet shirts were introduced by Revd Herbert Plater, headmaster 1854–93. Back row, far right is one of the Magnus' most famous pupils, Gonville Bromhead. During the Zulu Wars in 1879 he was awarded the VC for his part in the Battle of Rorke's Drift in defence of Natal.

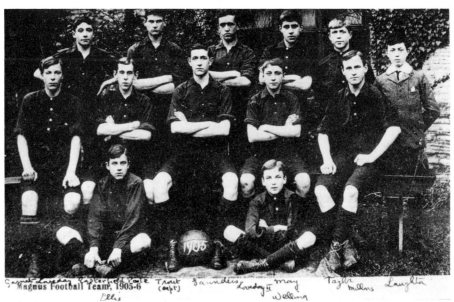

MAGNUS FOOTBALL TEAM, 1905/6. In c. 1911, under the headship of Henry Gorse, the school ceased playing football altogether. Since that date they have played only rugby. As early as 1913 the school magazine, the *Novarcensian*, reported 'Rugger has been voted an unqualified success by the whole school.'

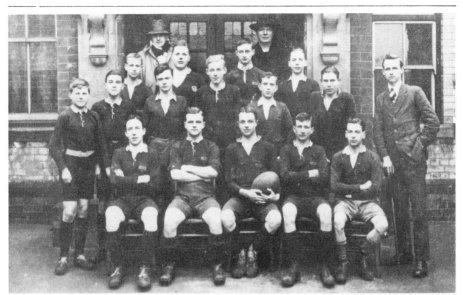

MAGNUS FIRST XV RUGBY TEAM, 1919. This picture features another famous Magnusian: (Sir) Donald Wolfit (second right, middle row) who, in the 1930s and '40s, became one of the country's foremost Shakespearian actors and the last of the great actor-managers. Also pictured is Albert Baker (sitting, first left).

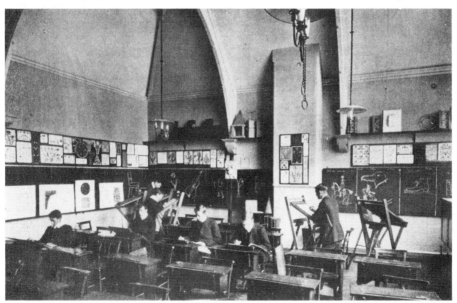

AN ART ROOM in the present Magnus buildings on Earp Avenue, c. 1911. In 1912 the school prospectus listed 120 day boys and 30 boarders. Fees were as follows: Day boys under 12, £7 p.a.; Day boys over 12, £8 p.a.; Boarders £42–48 p.a. Laundry was 10s. 6d. per term.

SHERWOOD FORESTERS ON PARADE AT THE MAGNUS. During the First World War the Sherwood Foresters (TA) Regiment shared the school field at Earp Avenue with the Magnus Cadet Corps (formed in 1915 by Mr Nickal). Donald Wolfit recalled, 'Boys would leave one term and show up at the beginning of the next as second lieutenants.' In the first year of war, 100 old Magnusians were serving around the world.

ST AUGUSTINE'S SCHOOL was originally held in St Augustine's Mission Room off Barnby Road. In 1906, under the Board School system, it found a permanent home in new purpose-built premises at what is now Barnby Road School. This group, simply known as 'St Augustine's School Group II', possibly dates from 1901–2.

THE AUSTERE MAIN HALL at Barnby Road School. The arches (far right) gave access to classrooms, while that at the far end led to the headmaster's office and (later) the school library.

CLASS 1 OF BARNBY ROAD COUNCIL SCHOOL, July 1912. The headmaster was Samuel A. Hildage while the mistress (possibly seen here) was Miss Clara Kitchen. Note the strict segregation of sexes in the seating arrangement.

NEWARK'S MOUNT SCHOOL on Mount Lane was set up in 1826. 101 years later this class of five-year-olds in 1927 features teacher Miss Veich (far right) and Edward Pinkney (middle row, fifth right). Highlight of the school year was the Mount School Treat given on breaking-up day before the August (Harvest) holidays.

CHRISTCHURCH SCHOOL FOOTBALL TEAM, 1933. Winners of both the Mumby Shield and Pratt Cup. Back row, left to right: W.E. Plummer, Mr Burden, H.E. Buttery, T.W. Smith, R.J. Henderson, Mr Niblett, T.E. Dalby. Front row: D.H. Berridge, L. Cliff (Captain), C. Mayfield, H. Rawson, K. Kay.

SECTION THREE

Work

WORKERS AT W.N. NICHOLSON & SONS TRENT IRONWORKS. William Newzam Nicholson established his firm in the 1840s. Noted for its agricultural machinery (principally 'horse rakes' and 'hay machines'), the factory also produced steam engines and bone crushing machines. The Trent Ironworks finally closed in 1968.

WORKERS AT ABBOTT & CO., hoist and boiler makers c. 1901.

WILLIAM CAFFERATA bought Beacon Hill quarry from the Newark Plaster Co. in 1858. Here at Hawton Quarry (opened 1881), we see gypsum quarrying by hand. Spoil was transported by wheelbarrow along 40 ft high walkways from the gypsum face (left) to the spoil heap (right). Surprisingly, the only man to fall escaped with a sprained ankle.

QUARRIED GYPSUM was loaded into railway wagons and taken to Hawton mineral mill. Seen here chopping gypsum by hand are, right to left: H. Bailey (nearest camera), M. Keane, C. Smalley, H. Booth, J. Saunders and T. Berridge.

CAFFERATA'S operated their own small railway between Hawton works and Beacon Hill quarry. Here, at Hawton in c. 1930, one of their Fowler locomotives (*Hilda*) gets under way with a train of trucks loaded with gypsum.

A BUSY RIVER SCENE AT NEWARK. Although water transport ultimately failed to compete with the railways, its decline was long and slow. This picture shows a still crowded Trent Navigation as late as 1930. The town's heyday as an inland port, however, had been more than a century earlier: in 1888 Newark handled over 6,500 barges.

THE MIDLAND WAS THE FIRST RAILWAY to reach Newark in August 1846. Although later eclipsed by the Great Northern, it was the Midland which graced Newark with superior ornament. Their classical Castle station, with unusual rounded ends, is today Grade II listed and boasts finely detailed pilasters on both entrance and platform sides.

Newark, Great
Northern Railway Station.

THE GREAT NORTHERN'S STATION at Northgate, opened in 1852, was much larger than the Midland's. A main line station, it featured a series of waiting rooms strictly segregated by sex and travelling class. This picture from 1907 shows the central refreshment rooms (now demolished) and the massive clock by W. Potts & Son of Leeds which still operates today.

ELIZABETH COX (second right) pictured with other workers from Gilstrap, Earp & Co.'s maltings. Much of Victorian Newark's wealth was founded in the malting industry. This picture dates from the First World War when women supplemented the workforce. For staffing purposes, two females equalled one male worker.

WORKERS FROM JAMES HOLE & CO.'S BREWERY, C. 1880s, outside the Trent warehouse. The central figure standing with bare feet is thought to be Charles Smith of Water Lane. The implements shown include wooden shovels for turning the malt.

DELIVERY CART FROM HOLE'S CASTLE BREWERY on Albert Street. Horses like this one, called 'Welsh Jack', were later replaced by bright yellow vans. Hole's won their gold medal in 1885 at the International Brewing Exhibition. Quality was attributed to the purity of water drawn from their 900 ft well.

MR A.J. ROBINSON, coal merchant, at the wheel of his delivery lorry. The firm began trading in the 1920s and ceased business in 1989 when the land they rented at Newark's Castle Station was sold to make way for the new cattle market.

A BRASS-BEDECKED HORSE used to pull Robinson's coal cart before motorization, pictured in the Castle Station yard. It is interesting to note that in this photograph the name of Robinsons' local rival, John Halstead of Castlegate, has been deleted from the railway wagons behind.

JAMES ANTCLIFF WIDDISON, coal merchant of no. 16 Friary Road, outside the Gilstrap Free Library on Castlegate at the turn of the century. Note the muddiness of the road.

THE LINCOLN ROAD GARAGE of Wright & Sons (now Travel Wright) in 1926. Established by Frank and Charles Wright as a motor repair and petrol sales business, they first ran 'bus services to Ossington, Laxton and Ollerton.

THE WRIGHT & SONS FLEET, having started with just two 'buses, soon expanded. Here in 1938, Mr and Mrs Wright stand proudly before one of their new Commer coaches.

SILVER QUEEN BUSES, now largely forgotten, used to provide the main 'bus link between Newark and Lincoln in the 1920s. Here, driver Bob Kirk is pictured at Bassingham, the half-way stage.

NEWARK VOLUNTEER CORPS at training camp near Newark, c. 1907. Among those 'spud-bashing' is Edward Pinkney. The 4th Newark Volunteers were formed in 1881 and disbanded shortly after this picture was taken (1908) when they became the 8th Territorial Battalion, Notts. & Derbys.

OFF TO WAR. Edward Pinkney, formerly of the Newark Volunteers, now a regular in the Sherwood Foresters, poses before heading for the Front in August 1914.

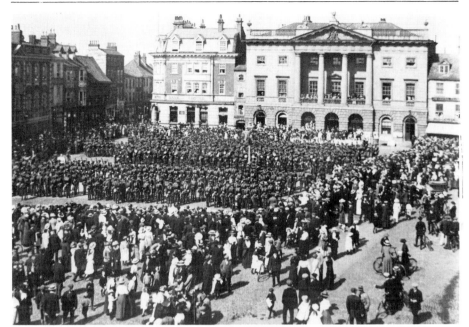

OFFICIAL FAREWELL to the 8th Battalion Sherwood Foresters upon their departure for France, 10 August 1914. In his address, the Mayor, J.C. Kew said, 'You go out from a town . . . which withstood onslaught and siege in days gone by, but whose brave defenders never tasted defeat . . . You will go forward with a baptism of their spirit.'

MUNITION WORKERS AT RANSOME & CO., ball-bearing manufacturers, First World War. Production of bearings was still very much in its infancy, yet to fight the new mechanized war they were needed in great quantities. As one of only five ball-bearing factories in the country, extra workers were drafted into Ransome's to boost output.

WORKERS FROM DAVID SLATER'S FISHING TACKLE MANUFACTORY on a factory outing, c. 1914–18, pictured in the castle grounds. Front row, left to right: Mr Garrand (foreman of works), Miss L. Hinchley, Edith Ebelthwaite, Annie King, Eleanor Beaumont, -?-, -?-, and Bob Ward. Middle row: Lorna Mills, -?-, Mrs Pulford, Ada Smith, -?-, -?-, -?-, Gladys Strutt.

WORKERS AT MILWARD & SONS LTD, fishing tackle manufacturers, Lombard Street, 1932. Among those pictured are Edie Ebelwhite and Betsy Curtis, while on the front row (third from left) is fourteen-year-old Jane Tharatt in her first job after leaving school.

OLDHAMS THE CATERERS was founded by John Eggleston in 1768. Included in this picture (taken in 1947 at Lord Brownlow's wedding in Grantham) are John Oldham (top left), and Mr Oldham sen. (middle, centre). Back row: Nell King (seventh from left), Edna Martin (tenth left) and Dorothy Cox (thirteenth left).

MR R.A. SHELDRAKE, chemist, in his shop at no. 43 Appletongate, 1920s. Much of the shop's contents are now preserved in the Millgate Folk Museum in Newark.

JOSEPH HALL, newsagent of no. 37 Balder-tongate, was Town Crier in Newark for twenty-nine years between 1896 and 1925. He is photographed here in 1901.

BERT HALL, who succeeded his father, Joseph, as Town Crier, held office between 1925 and 1951. Likewise listed in Newark's trade directories as a newsagent and clockmaker, Bert Hall also bore the distinction of being a fine amateur pianist, conjuror and comedian.

BERT HALL'S 'AUCTION TENT' – another of his sidelines – may well have caught the eye of Newarkers visiting Mablethorpe in the 1930s. Here he sold such items as watches, clocks, cutlery and jewellery. Bert is pictured outside the tent with his daughter, Cissie.

YET A THIRD GENERATION OF HALLS became Town Crier in 1951 when Bert Hall was succeeded by his son, Bert (jun.). He was Town Crier for thirty-three years until 1984. Here he is wearing the ceremonial uniform, made-to-measure by Rick's outfitters at the not inconsiderable cost of £470.

THE STALL OF J. MATHER & CO. (automobile, electrical, heating and agricultural engineers) at Wollaton Show, 10–14 July 1928. Among the machinery on show are examples from local manufacturers such as Ransome's and Nicholson's. Fifteen years before this picture was taken (in 1903), Mather had been joined in the business by Mr J.L. Maltby.

MR J.L. MALTBY was 70 years old when the Mather-Maltby partnership came to an end in 1933. Yet instead of retiring Mr Maltby opened his own business and, moreover, continued to play an active part in it until his death aged 96. The business continues to flourish to this day.

A GROUP OF NEWARK'S 'NIGHT SOIL' COLLECTORS enjoy a glass of beer during a break in their round. Before the widespread introduction of domestic water closets and main sewers, earth closets had to be emptied 'by hand'. Believed to have been photographed in the Bowbridge Road area, this picture includes William Pratt (far left).

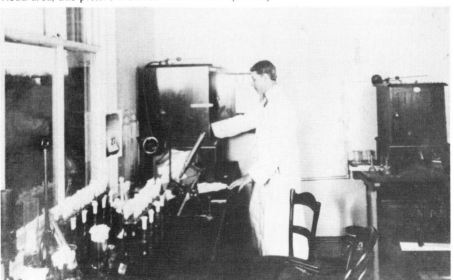

MR ERNEST PARNHAM, agricultural chemists analyst, working in the laboratories of Quibell Brothers, 1906. Quibell's, seedsmen, oil cake merchants and chemical manure, sheep dip and glue manufacturers, were taken over by Croda who continue the making of glue.

NEWARK BOROUGH POLICE in the castle grounds, January 1933. Back row, left to right: P.C. Morley, P.C. Parkin. Second row: P.C. Newbury, P.C. Flowers, P.C. Smith, P.C. Philipson, P.C. Tomlinson. Third row: Acting Sergeant Smith, P.C. Brown, P.C. Armstrong, P.C. Hurt, P.C. Wood, P.C. Coe. Front row: Sergeant Francis, Sergeant Millhouse, James McConnach (Chief Constable), Sergeant Griffin, Sergeant Kemp.

MR MOUNTNEY, a familiar figure at the turn of the century, seen here feeding the castle pigeons. He kept a small 'museum' in the castle which included such curios as Roman pottery, a copy of the Magna Carta, cannon balls dredged from the Trent, and 'a model of the moon done in beeswax'.

SECTION FOUR

Recreation

NEWARK'S PALACE THEATRE was developed on the Chauntry House site by Mrs Emily Blagg and opened on 5 July 1920. The opening programme featured the silent movie classic *King Solomon's Mines* accompanied by full orchestra. Pictured here in 1924, posters advertise Buster Keaton's film *The Navigator*.

NEWARK ACQUIRED A NEW CINEMA in 1935 – the Savoy on Middlegate. The *Newark Advertiser* welcomed the scheme wholeheartedly as a competitor to the Palace and pointed out that, in those dark years of the Depression, '... any new enterprise which means work and wages is to be welcomed in our midst'.

THE INTERIOR OF THE SAVOY takes shape. Heralded as a 'Super Cinema' it had seating for 1,500 picture-goers. Among those seen here erecting the balcony is Mr Lewis Smith.

NEWARK'S BEST REMEMBERED CHIEF LIBRARIAN at the Gilstrap is Arthur Smith (front, centre) who held the post for 41 years between 1919 and 1960. Pictured here in 1933, he is surrounded by his staff. Standing, left to right: Edmund Fryer, Christopher Haywood, G.U.S. Selby, -?-. Seated: Ian Clark, Arthur Smith, Frederick Baines.

THE REFERENCE LIBRARY in 1921. The portrait by local artist W.H. Cubley of Sir William Gilstrap, who gave the library to the town, is a prominent feature. At one time there were no less than sixteen 'Silence' notices dotted around the building – quite a contrast with the welcoming air of today's modern glass library in Beaumond Gardens.

LIBRARY ASSISTANT JANET BRAY pictured inside a newly commissioned Gilstrap Mobile Library van, 1950s. Mobile library services began in Newark in 1958 and continue to serve outlying rural communities to this day.

THE VICTORIA INN, previously known as the Marquis of Granby, at no. 61 Baldertongate was leased by George Heppenstall in 1860. Between c. 1922 and 1950 the landlord was Wilfred L. Shotwell who is pictured here. During recent renovation, timbering, possibly dating from the sixteenth century, was found beneath the brickwork.

THE START OF NEWARK'S ANNUAL JULY HOLIDAY WEEK caused such an exodus to the seaside that additional Lincolnshire Road Car 'buses had to be brought over from Lincoln to cope with the rush. Here in c. 1936 the white-coated relief drivers are, left to right: Mrs Askenhurst, Herbert Turner, Bill Cook and Albert Beale.

MEMBERS OF PARLIAMENT STREET PRIMITIVE METHODIST CHURCH in costume for a performance of the 'operetta' *Pearl and the Fishmaiden*, c. 1922. Back row, left to right: Jim Barrett, Martha Files, William Riley. Middle row: Doris Smith, -?-, Fred Riley (with beard), Dulcie Lane. Front row: Eileen Riley, -?-, Nessie Lane.

A DISPLAY OF DIVING marks the opening of the open-air swimming baths on Sherwood Avenue in 1934.

A VIEW OF THE ENTIRE POOL showing diving boards, slide (left) and the fine 1930s neo-classical changing rooms (now demolished). When this photograph was taken (c. 1959) entrance fees were 9d. for adults and 4d. for children.

THE CHILDREN'S PADDLING POOL, situated beside the main adult pool, shown here in the mid-1930s.

SWIMMING IN THE RIVER TRENT OFF TOLNEY LANE. Before the Sherwood Avenue baths were built, Newarkers did their bathing in the Trent. In this view (dating from 1909) the bathers are watched over by swimming instructor and superintendent Samuel Warren Taylor who is standing on the boards with his back to the camera.

NEWARK'S ANNUAL MAY FAIR has welcomed the summer for more than 1,000 years. When this picture was taken, c. 1903, May Fair was held in the Market Place. It later moved to a paddock on London Road and then to Tolney Lane.

SIX FAIRS WERE HELD ANNUALLY, originally for the sale of horses, cattle, sheep and pigs. Although trade is still represented in the top picture by Mills' basket stall, by 1903 the main purpose of the May Fair was popular amusement.

TOWN CRIER BERT HALL quietens the crowd in preparation for Mr W.E. Knight (former Mayor and Freeman of the Borough) to proclaim May Fair 1934 open. Also assembled on the steps of J.W. Proctor's roundabout are the Mayor, Alderman G. Stephenson, Councillor Staniland and Councillor Ernest Randall.

NEWARK SALVATION ARMY BAND, 1910, outside their then headquarters at the Old Wool Hall on Millgate. The side drum was played by W. Cunnington, bass drum by bandsman Swallow, and trombone (second left) by F. Willows. The bandmaster was Mr Campion.

NEWARK CIVIL DEFENCE DARTS TEAM, 1942. On the back row (far left) is Irving Lewin and Frank Crouch (fourth from left), while in the centre with the cup is Harry Reed. Although obviously a winning team, the nature of their victory appears lost in history.

MAJOR HUGH HOLE (first Newark District Commissioner) with the 5th Newark Scout Group's mascot, two-year-old Albert Gilbert. This photograph was taken in 1921, at the entrance to Sconce Hills. Although fully kitted-out, Albert never actually became a scout.

NEWARK ROWING CLUB. Fresh from winning the 'Maiden 4s' trophy at Ross-on-Wye on August Bank Holiday 1930, the team from Newark Rowing Club are back on familiar territory on the River Devon at Farndon. They are, left to right: Colin Webster (stroke), Fred Harpham, Ronald Hanns, George Jessop and Ronald Edwards.

NEWARK BOWLING CLUB laid out the green on London Road in 1809. The pavilion, with its fascinating mixture of classical and local architecture, bears the inscription 'Let no Man be biased' – a cry for fair play. For over a hundred years after its inception the club team never lost on home ground.

MR W.T. POSTLES, amateur sprint champion of the Midlands displaying his trophies in the back yard of his Appletongate home, c. 1910. The son of a gardener at the Friary and an employee at Abbott & Co. boiler makers, he also played for Newark Town football club.

NEWARK FOOTBALL CLUB, formed in 1868, is believed to be the fourth oldest club in England. Matches were first played on the Grove ground at Balderton, although by the time this picture was taken (1907–8) they had moved to a field off the Muskham Road.

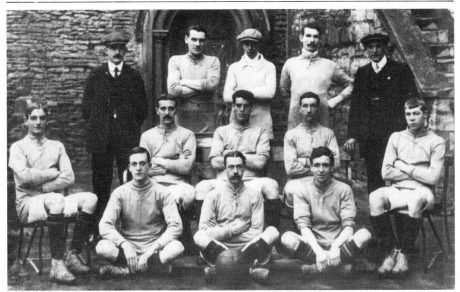

NEWARK TOWN FOOTBALL CLUB photographed in the castle grounds in 1910. Back row, left to right: W. Sills (Hon. Treasurer), T. Angus, L. Robinson, W. Aldridge, -?-. Middle row: A. Hall, W. Weselby, J. Bryan (capt.), A. Bentley, -?-. Front row: H. Hedefine, W. Postles, E. Knighton.

WAKES & LAMBS FOOTBALL CLUB, 1910/11. This successful football team were champions of the Newark and District League, joint holders of the Newark League Challenge Cup, and winners of the Newark Hospital Cup. Back row, left to right: H. Trollope, H. Lamb (Hon. Sec.), C. Mellors, H. Crampton, W. Lunn (Capt.), W.W. Lamb, J. Parker (trainer). Middle row: R. Bentley, W. Burton, T. Rowbottom, R. Hayes. Front row: F. Riley (kneeling), F.E. Smith (Vice-Capt.), P. Harrison, C. Keetley, H. Doncaster (kneeling).

ST LEONARD'S CHURCH FOOTBALL CLUB, 1922. Among the players are Jim Riley (second left, back row) and Jim Barrett (third left, back row). The Revd Alfred Parkinson, vicar of St Leonard's, is also present.

NEWARK YMCA GYM TEAM, 1931. Back row, left to right: W. Osmond, A. Clarkstone, A. Johnson, A.F. Wilson, F. Keeton, R. Lowe, J. Grosse, F. Hoddinott (instructor). Middle row: J. Wilkinson, W. Setchfield, J. H. Woodall (Gen. Sec.) H. Brown, J. Wright. Front row: G. Geeson, A. Priestly, A. Brake, J. Parr, W. Nix.

NEWARK MOTOR CYCLE CLUB pictured at a local 'reliability' trial, 2 June 1923. Ninth from the right is Mr L.R. Hutchinson, one of the club's stalwarts. Also pictured are Joe Longdon and Bill Donald of Donald's Garage which used to be on London Road.

A GROUP OF NEWARK MOTORISTS, parked outside Mather's garage on Lombard Street. Although the location is clear, the purpose of their gathering remains a mystery. It has been suggested that the picture dates from c. 1914 to 1918 owing to what appears to be a gas bag on top of the last car – a result of petrol shortage?

THE CHOIR OF ST AUGUSTINE'S CHURCH in 1937, here pictured outside the London Road home of William Becher Tidd Pratt (middle row, centre). Pratt was mayor no less than seven times and was one of Newark's great benefactors: he gave the 'Stadium' football ground to the schoolboys of the town.

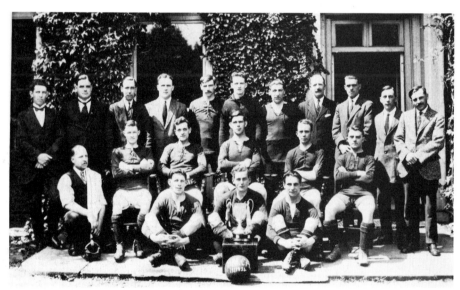

NEWARK YMCA FOOTBALL CLUB, 1923/4, winners of the Newark League championship and runners-up in the Challenge and Hospital cups. Back row, left to right: F. Cobb (Chairman), J.H. Woodhall (Gen. Sec.), J. Green (Treasurer), S. Morley, A Bagaley, W. Speirs, V. Lunn (Vice-capt.), F. Smith, C. Hopewell, J. Turner (Secretary), A. Setchfield (Vice Chairman). Middle row: W. Grocock, W. Weselby, P. Andrews, W. Maull, E. Asman. Front row: W. Marshall (Trainer), J. Graveney, D. Mort, J. Grosse (Captain).

NEWARK'S ANNUAL SUNDAY SCHOOL TREAT was held the third Thursday (later Saturday) in June. Floats (or 'devices') assembled in pre-ordained order in the market place to be judged for inventiveness and splendour. Taken in 1939 this picture shows one of the largest Sunday school treats. They virtually ceased after the war.

DEVICES FROM LOCAL CHURCHES AND CHAPELS were judged according to three categories, A, B, or C. Category A was for religious themes, and here, in 1927, we see the Class A entry from Newark Salvation Army school, 'Samson breaking the pillars of the temple' with John Bull as Samson.

'ELIJAH AND THE WIDOW'S SON', another Class A device, this time from Charles Street Methodist Sunday school, won second prize.

CLASS B DEVICES FEATURED NON-RELIGIOUS THEMES. Here, Charles Street Methodists won second prize in c. 1937 for their Class B entry 'If I were a boy again'. Pictured on the wagon are Jack Hardy (behind tent) and Jack Dring (sitting). Standing left of the wagon are Owen Robb (far right) and Laurie Bryan (with hat).

CLASS C DEVICES CONSISTED OF ORDINARY WAGONS for junior members. In 1907 Charles Street Methodists produced this remarkable swan for their Class C entry. At the reins is Mr Reginald Sheldrake.

CHARLES STREET METHODISTS also produced this magnificent wheeled model of Newark Castle in that same year (1907).

UNKNOWN CLASS C DEVICE outside Baines building contractor's yard, Lombard Street, 1890s.

UNKNOWN CLASS C DEVICE, Newark market place, 1920s.

CERTIFICATES WERE ALSO AWARDED FOR BEST GROOMED HORSE. Here, in c. 1936, the horse belonging to Jack Bailey, coal merchant of Victoria Street, has won 4th prize pulling Parliament Street Methodists' device. Standing with the horse is Mr William Atkinson, carter for Claypole flour mill.

AFTER JUDGING WAS OVER the devices paraded around the town, preceded by children with garlands of flowers. Pictured here among the procession in 1938 or 1939 is Jean Ragsdale (third from left).

THE KING AND QUEEN OF THE TREAT, played here in 1939 by Mr John 'Bo' Woodall and Mr Taylor.

THE PROCESSION ENDED AT SCONCE HILLS. Here races were run on the Bottom Hills while on the Top Hills competitions in skipping (seen here), singing and performing 'Action Songs' were held on a central wooden platform. To make the day complete, each child was given a ticket which could be exchanged for a bun and lemonade.

SECTION FIVE

Shopping

NEWARK MARKET is held four days a week in one of the largest cobbled squares in the country. Putting aside changes in dress and the passing of horse-drawn transport, this photograph of c. 1900 depicts a scene still eminently recognizable to any Newarker today.

MR WALTER SMITH, grocer and tea dealer, outside his shop at 19 Market Place, c. 1890. Smith's are listed in Newark's trade directories from the mid-1860s to c. 1920 when the premises were acquired by G.H. Porter's and run in tandem with their celebrated Bridge Street store. Here, Pipers Penny Bazaar occupies the adjacent frontage.

GEORGE HOWARD PORTER took over the grocery business at no. 1 Bridge Street in c. 1893–4. It remained in the Porter family until 1968 when the then manager, Mr Peter Speirs, took over. The building itself is notable as the former premises of C.J. Ridge, printer, who published Byron's first poems in 1806.

MR CLAUDE KING of Clews furniture shop, Stodman Street, addresses Newark tradesmen from the town hall steps, c. 1942. Second right is Mr G.H. Porter, while his son, Stanley G. Porter (with rosette) stands beside Mrs Parlby of the WVS. Behind them stands Bert Hall (Town Crier), and immediately right of the speaker is Dr D.C. Hine.

JOSEPH STRAY bought his 'animal feed emporium' at the corner of Boar Lane and Middlegate at auction in July 1904. He continued as proprietor until his death in 1945 when the business was taken over by his son. Stray's continues to flourish today.

JOHN COTTAM BAINBRIDGE, draper and 'funeral furnisher', bought the Old White Hart in 1867. The long, glass third floor frontage proved ideal for dressmaking, and here Bainbridge employed girls – often as young as 14 – as sempstresses and milliners. In c. 1900 the business was taken over by Charles and Frederick Atter who developed the adjacent Arcade.

SEWING-ROOM STAFF, BAINBRIDGES, 1915. Front row, right to left: Mabel Streeton and Anne Atkinson (sitting). Immediately behind sits Ethel Merrin, while second left (standing) is Mabel May Sooby. Their 'uniform' comprised navy serge skirts and white blouses. At all times during the working day (8 a.m. – 8 p.m.) they were instructed to address each other as 'Miss'.

MR JOHN MILLS OF MILLS & SONS LTD, bootmakers (est. 1858), with the largest solid leather boot in the world, manufactured by his company in 1887 for the Newark Tradesmen's procession at Queen Victoria's Golden Jubilee celebrations. Measuring 4 ft 3 in from heel to toe, the boot contained 470 in of hand stitching.

THE MONSTER BOOT GIVEN PRIDE OF PLACE in Mills' shop window, no. 11 Middlegate. Mills & Sons also had outlets on Bridge Street and at King Street, Southwell.

WILLIAM MARCH (centre, doorway) with his three assistants or live-in apprentices. March operated his chemist business at no. 5 Market Place from c. 1851. In 1880 George Widdowson Cherrington was appointed manager, and eventually took over the business completely. It is his name which still appears above the shop today.

CHARLES A. BRUNNING established his business in 1842 and held the site at no. 36 Kirkgate until 1973. One-time 'art florist' and fruiterer, Brunning's main trade was as a seedsman. From nurseries on Appletongate he was proud to advertise the dependability of his garden seeds.

JOHN PRATT (far right), game dealer, no. 5 Cartergate, C. 1900. From top to bottom his display comprises rabbits, hares (two rows), turkeys, ducks and geese, pheasants and wet fish. Pictured far left is James Watson who killed and cleaned the game. Just visible behind Mr Pratt is his son, Frank, who later fitted a generator behind the shop to provide electric light. So many other firms asked him to help them enter the electric age that he formed the business that became Pratt & Gelsthorpe Ltd on Baldertongate.

EDWARDS THE TAILORS, no. 42 Stodman Street. Pictured here is Mr Alfred Ronald Edwards, proprietor and master tailor, grandson of the founder, Mr Thomas Edwards, who had started the business on Castlegate in 1864.

BRADLEYS CLOTHIERS AND OUTFITTERS at nos 51–52 Stodman Street. Photographed in 1950 it is interesting to note the display of early television sets in Kelsall's window next door.

T. RICHMOND & SON, cooper, cask and churn manufacturers of Boar Lane, Newark, pictured at Newark Agricultural Show, c. 1890. Mr Thomas Richmond is seen leaning on the trellis (left). In the foreground is one of the company's principal products, a hand operated butter churn.

RICHMOND'S SHOP, known as 'The Cooperage', was at no. 4 Boar Lane. Pictured in 1915 is the proprietor, Mr Raymond Leigh Richmond (sans cap). Richmond's sold a wide variety of goods including straw bee-hives, washing machines, mangles and wringers, hair and wire sieves, corn and chaff sieves, malt shovels and butchers' trays. They also smoked hams to order.

WOOLWORTHS CAME TO NEWARK amid a flurry of anticipation in 1932. 'The premises [on Stodman Street]', reported the *Newark Advertiser*, 'will be demolished and rebuilt. The interior will be 32 ft wide and 156 ft long ... This will make a room nearly twice the size of the town hall'. Woolworths finally departed – much lamented – in 1984.

A FINE DISPLAY OF CLOCHE HATS in Jacksons millinery and shoe shop at the corner of St Marks Lane and Stodman Street in 1931. St Marks Lane used to lead to a maze of back alleys and a covered market. This has now been swept away by a modern shopping precinct.

J.W. WHITE'S GROCERY SHOP on Portland Street stood next to the Portland Arms (far right). Pictured here, c. 1900, with Mr White are (far left) Edward William White (son of proprietor) and shop boy Harry Toule. Edward White later opened his own grocery business on Barnbygate (see below).

EDWARD WILLIAM WHITE'S GROCERY SHOP on the corner of Charles Street and Barnbygate, c. 1920. He also owned the model bakery opposite the shop at no. 183 Barnbygate. This picture shows Miss C.M. Robinson and a young George Edward White (son of the proprietor). The shop is now a second-hand store.

OPENING THE CO-OP FOODSTORE ON KIRKGATE, 1938. Performing the ceremony is Mr Wilson, President of the Newark Co-operative Society (right), accompanied by Mr Frederick Paine, Managing Secretary of the Newark Society. Immediately to the right of Mr Wilson is Trevor Wadsworth a reporter on the *Newark Advertiser* taking notes for his column.

FRONTAGE OF NEWARK CO-OP'S KIRKGATE STORE, photographed shortly after the official opening (compare window displays). Above shop height the main façade (dated 1937) remains little changed today although, through amalgamation with the Lincoln Co-operative Society, the store has expanded into several of the adjacent premises.

NEWARK CO-OPERATIVE SOCIETY BAKERY was on Lovers Lane. Here, senior members of the society and bakery workers pose for a photograph at the opening ceremony.

THE NOTTINGHAM FIRM OF BOOTS came to Newark in the mid-1890s and still occupies the same Stodman Street site today. Pictured here in 1930, their 'Book Lovers Library' – an offshoot of the book sales department – was already well established.

MR ROBERT MACKENDER, nurseryman, seedsman, and bee appliance dealer, outside his shop at no. 43 Northgate, late 1920s. An accomplished apiarist himself, Mr Mackender kept his hives behind the shop.

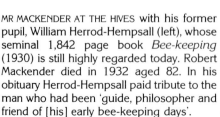

MR MACKENDER AT THE HIVES with his former pupil, William Herrod-Hempsall (left), whose seminal 1,842 page book *Bee-keeping* (1930) is still highly regarded today. Robert Mackender died in 1932 aged 82. In his obituary Herrod-Hempsall paid tribute to the man who had been 'guide, philosopher and friend of [his] early bee-keeping days'.

SECTION SIX

Memorable Events

King Edward in his Motor Car passing over Trent Bridge, Newark, 14th September, 1905

EDWARD VII PASSED THROUGH NEWARK on his way from Rufford Abbey (where he was the house guest of Lord Savile) to Belvoir Castle. The *Newark Herald* commented favourably on the king's 'handsome and luxuriously appointed 40hp Mercedes' and noted that his route through the town had been specially swept and watered prior to his arrival.

'Sandy.' The bird taking corn from the persons mouth is th
ne which alighted on the shoulder of H.M. KING EDWARD VI.
in his visit to flewark Castle in Sept 1909.

EDWARD VII VISITED NEWARK AGAIN in September 1909, this time making a surprise visit to the castle. 'Newarkers were agog with pleasurable excitement and on the tip-toe of expectation' reported the *Newark Advertiser*. The king was conducted round by the castle keeper, Mr Mountney, seen here in a highly original commemorative postcard.

ONLY A YEAR LATER EDWARD VII WAS DEAD. Here the Town Clerk, Godfrey Tallents, surrounded by the Mayor, Alderman F.H. Appleby, and the corporation, stands on the official proclamation stool on Beastmarket Hill to announce the succession of George V, on 10 May 1910.

DECORATIONS IN CARTERGATE to celebrate the coronation of George V, 22 June 1911. Note Beaumond Cross in its original position (right) and Harrison & Co.'s garage (left). Newark's coronation celebrations cost £400, and this arch won the first prize of £5 in the triumphal arch and illuminations competition.

GEORGE V VISITED NEWARK on 9 July 1928. Arriving at Northgate station, he was met by the Mayor, C.H. Dale, and Major Hugh Tallents DSO, Town Clerk. The *Newark Advertiser* reported 'splendid evidence on every hand that the inhabitants of Newark were animated by a spirit of loyalty and affection for their Sovereign . . .'.

GEORGE V AND QUEEN MARY in the castle grounds, 9 July, 1928. On the left of the Queen are Cllr C.H. Dale (Mayor), Col R.F.B. Hodgkinson, Major H. Tallents (Town Clerk). Right of the King are Viscount Galway, Sir Lancelot and Lady Maud Rolleston, Sir Ernest Jardine Bt, Mr K.T. Meaby and Col and Mrs Lemon.

MRS FLORENCE KNIGHT'S WOOL SHOP, no. 19 Cartergate, decorated to celebrate the coronation of King George VI on 13 May 1937. In Newark the coronation service at St Mary's was timed to allow the congregation to return home and hear the investiture broadcast live from Westminster Abbey on the wireless.

THE FOUNDER OF THE SALVATION ARMY, General William Booth, visited Newark on 30 July 1909 – just three years before his death aged 84. He is pictured here with the Mayor and Mrs Oliver Quibell on the steps of their home, Shalom Lodge (now part of Lilley & Stone School) on London Road.

MEMBERS OF CHARLES STREET METHODIST CHURCH put out the flags for the stone-laying of their new building on 6 July 1905. Originally established in 1885 to help poor families in the area, by 1905 the church had proved so successful that larger premises were needed. The new building cost £1,115.

THE FLOODS OF MAY 1932. A view southwards from the castle showing the chimney of the Trent Brewery (far left) and Parnham's flour mill (left centre). Parnham's mill was gutted by fire in 1965 and the site is now occupied by the Severn Trent boat yard.

FLOODING AT BRITISH SUGAR'S FACTORY on Kelham Road, 1947. The picture shows the packaging plant (far left) and, behind the boat, the fitting shop. Standing behind the boat (in light suit) is Jack Toynbee (beet end foreman), while Jim Bailey (pulp stones chargehand) is standing on the far right in front of the stores.

THE LAST FREEZE OF THE TRENT occured in January 1895. Although these local inhabitants, photographed under Mill Bridge at the end of Mill Lane, appear perfectly at ease, several fatalities due to thin ice were reported in the area.

HAILSTORM AT NEWARK. The morning of 11 July 1903 was stiflingly hot with the thermometer reaching 110° F. Storm clouds gathered in the afternoon and, driven by a northerly gale, rained hailstones of up to one inch across on to the town. Recording the extraordinary event, this postcard shows damage to the Methodist New Connexion chapel on Barnbygate.

AVIATION MEETING PROMOTED BY MR. JOHN MATHER, MOTOR & AEROPLANE AGENT, NEWARK-ON-TRENT. MR. BROCK FLYING OVER THE COURSE, MAY 15, 1913.

A DEPRESSION MONOPLANE flying over Newark, 15 May 1913. As promotor, Mr Mather naturally wished to be the first passenger in the plane. 'But', the *Newark Advertiser* reported, because 'he [was] rather heavy . . . [the pilot] . . . declined to take the risk straight away.' By removing some of his clothes, however, the ascent was made and John Mather became the first Newarker to fly over the town.

AN UNGAINLY CIERVA 'AUTOGIRO' (piloted by Capt. Schofield) was among the planes on show in May 1931, when the record-breaking long distance pilot Capt. C.D. Barnard visited Newark with his 'Air Circus'. A forerunner of today's helicopters, the 'autogiro's' vertical ascents were a great novelty then, adding to the upsurge of interest shown in air travel in the 1930s.

'THE WHOLE TOWN OF NEWARK was brill-
iantly illuminated by the leaping flames
of a huge fire which broke out last night
at the maltkilns of Messrs Gilstrap, Earp
& Co., Northgate ... Windows in the
vicinity reflected the flames like a hundred mirrors and sparks festooned
themselves in the sky like flying rock-
ets.' *Newark Advertiser* 2.4.1930.

THE MORNING AFTER at Gilstrap, Earp & Co.'s maltkilns. The Price family, scrap dealers of
Newark, are scouring the ruins for salvage. Left to right: Ernie Price, William Price
(proprietor), Fred Price, Timothy Price, Matt Smith, Billy Smith, George Price, Tim Price.

OFFICIAL OPENING OF THE GILSTRAP LIBRARY EXTENSION, 2 August 1933. Pictured here are Miss Gilstrap, the Mayor Dr Ernest Ringrose and Mr Jast of the library committee. Now no longer needed as a library, the building has become the town's Tourist Information Centre.

THE MATERNITY WING AT NEWARK HOSPITAL was opened on 7 October 1937 by the Marchioness of Titchfield. Seen here also are Lord Titchfield (speaking), the Mayor, P.J.C. Staniland, Archdeacon of Newark (Ven. J.P. Hales), Chaplain (Canon A. Parkinson), the Matron (Miss Cottrill) and, in top hat, Thomas Turgoose, mace-bearer and town hall keeper.

FRESH WATER BEING SENT VIA THE MIDLAND RAILWAY from Newark to Lincoln, in 1905, during a typhoid outbreak there. Today it is hard to believe that less than 100 years ago mass epidemics such as typhoid were not an uncommon occurrence in this country.

GRACIE FIELDS visiting Ransome & Marles' ball-bearing factory during the Second World War. The local newspapers (subject to reporting restrictions) did not record the event, but it is thought probable that the visit was a morale-booster after the bombing of R&M's in March 1941.

THE FESTIVAL OF BRITAIN, 1951, was celebrated locally with a week-long programme of events. On 28 June the specially commissioned Festival Gates at the castle grounds were opened by the Mayor, J.A. Markwick. Here, Mrs Markwick receives a bunch of flowers while the Town Crier, Bert Hall, looks on.

A PERFORMANCE OF 'MERRIE ENGLAND', staged in the castle grounds by Newark Amateur Operatic Society and other local groups, was the highlight of Newark's Festival of Britain celebrations. Here, Gerda Pinkney plays 'Girl all alone' and James Woodward 'Long Tom' in a shot taken during rehearsals.

ON THE FIRST SUNDAY IN THE NEW MAYORAL YEAR the Mayor and Aldermen of Newark attend divine service at the parish church. Here, at the 'Mayor's Sunday Parade' of November 1951, the Mayor, J.A. Markwick, is flanked (left) by Thomas Turgoose (Mayors' Officer) and (right) by Bert Hall (Town Crier).

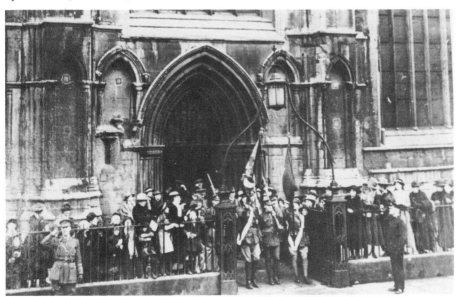

ARMISTICE CELEBRATIONS, marching out with the colours. This picture is thought to be of the tenth anniversary service held in St Mary's on 11 November 1928 – a doubly formal occasion as it coincided with the Mayor's Sunday.

THE PAGEANT OF NEWARK was staged in the castle grounds between 13 and 18 July 1936. In nightly performances, lasting three hours, 2,000 local residents re-enacted key moments from Newark's past: from Paulinus' visit in AD 600, through the death of King John, the Civil War, Byron's first poems, to W.E. Gladstone's election as the town's MP in 1832.

NEWARK PAGEANT. Each performance was opened by a local dignitary. On 16 July, however, the show was opened (via the trans-Atlantic radio telephone) by the Mayor of Newark, New Jersey, the Hon. Meyer C. Ellenstein. Here, left to right: E.J. Casterton (P.O. Radio-Telephony Dept), Cllr C.W. Jenkinson, D. Dwyre (American Consul-General) and P.J.C. Staniland (Mayor).

NEWARK PAGEANT. A collection of principal characters in Newark's history. Back row: Dr Arderne (H.W. Mace), Gopher (R. Burden), Bishop Warburton (S.R. Mogford), Col Staunton (Capt. Oliver), -?-. Front row: Dr. Blow (R.J. Corner), John Lilley (R.G. Walker), Henry Stone (T.A. Dobbs), Jennie Deans (Miss D.M. Creighton), Dr Pierson (Revd R. Holme).

NEWARK PAGEANT. At about the time Thomas Magnus endowed Newark Grammar School (1532), Cardinal Wolsey, disgraced at court, passed through the town and the two met. Here Wolsey is played by John 'Bo' Woodall, his page by J.A. Ridge. The part of Archdeacon Magnus was shared by two performers, J. Potter and J. Barker.

NEWARK PAGEANT. Pikemen in Wolsey's procession,

NEWARK PAGEANT. Ladies-in-waiting from the court of Queen Elizabeth. Fourth left is Joyce Elliot, while fifth left is Isobella Markham.

NEWARK PAGEANT. The Civil War episode was produced by Newark Technical College. Here we see J. Greatorex as King Charles I and E.R. Latham as Prince Rupert. Numerous animals were used in the Pageant and had to be penned overnight. One night they escaped and horses, sheep and goats had to be chased along Castlegate.

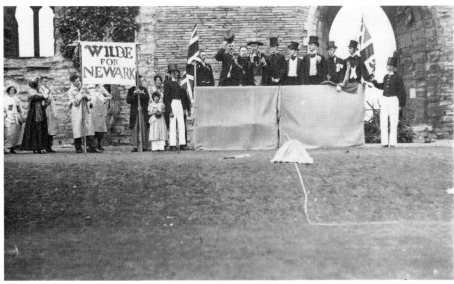

NEWARK PAGEANT. The Mayor (E.G. Walker) declares the election of William Ewart Gladstone (C.D. Maxon, first right of Mayor without hat) as Conservative MP for Newark (1832) over Mr Sergeant Wilde (R. Robertson) and William Farnworth Handley (G. Lord).

REMEMBERING THE PAGEANT, fifty years on, Mrs Ruth Blatherwick (whose husband, Douglas Blatherwick, had been the prime mover) recalled, 'For a whole week Newark lived in a different atmosphere. The streets were alive in the evening with people in period costume. You could meet a Saxon herdsman, an Elizabethan courtier, a Civil War soldier or Gladstone.'

Around Newark

MAIN STREET, BALDERTON, looking south with the spire of St Giles church and blacksmithy (centre, left). The small boy with the bag is Bill Ghent who, later in life, wrote a history of Balderton. He was an inspector at Ransome & Marles ball-bearing manufactory in Newark and, for many years, a parish councillor in Balderton.

AERIAL VIEW FROM THE SPIRE OF ST GILES' CHURCH, Balderton. In the left foreground is Joseph Knott's bakery (extant 1824–1966). Today the houses of Knott's Court stand on this site. A short way up Bullpit Lane is the bakehouse (with white roof), while opposite Knott's (right foreground) stands the Old Cock Inn.

THE MAYOR OF NEWARK, A.E. Whomsley, re-opening Balderton Co-op on London Road in 1950, following extensions and refurbishment.

MONTY WELLS' HORSE-DRAWN OMNIBUS, Balderton, c. 1902. Mr Wells (at the reins) is listed as carrier (Wednesdays and Saturdays) between Balderton and Newark. His route terminated at the Castle and Falcon in Newark where he would also pick up people and small goods for the return journey.

THE MACHINE SHOP at the Lowfield works of Worthington-Simpson, Balderton pump manufacturers, c. 1920. Pictured with parts for a pumping station in Buenos Aires is Herbert Bennett.

GIBSON'S CHARITY SCHOOL, Balderton, was erected in 1846 by the Revd William Smithson. Children were educated for 1d. per week. The building is now St Giles' church hall. This picture of pupils features George Arthur Shipman who was born in 1893. This gives a probable date for the picture as c. 1898.

'THE GYPSIES': pupils from Balderton School on stage at Newark Technical College, c. 1934. Back row, left to right: Frank Gale, Ted Fairhall, Frank Ifold. Middle row: Dennis Johnson, Linda Marshall, -?-, Nora Young, Joyce Binns, Lesley Hadfield, Vera Johnson. Front row: -?-, Reg Dixon, Winnie Thomas, -?-, -?-, Jack Calcroft, Frances Fell.

BALDERTON'S FIRST FOOTBALL TEAM, c. 1893. Officials of the club (not pictured) included Mr A. Warwick (President), Revd J. Farmer and Mr W.D. Warwick (Vice Presidents). The Hon. Sec. and Treasurer was Mr H. Wilkinson and the Asst Sec., Mr J. James. It is thought the team are pictured outside the old vicarage on London Road (now demolished).

METHODIST WOMEN'S MONDAY MEETING, Balderton, c. 1916. Back row, left to right: Freda Wallace, Emma Smithson, Mrs Rowbottom, Mrs Green, Mrs Johnson, Mrs Brown, Mrs Lord, Mrs Saunders. Front row: Mrs Gent, Mrs Padgett, Mrs Bailey, Mrs Wild, Sister Kate White, Mrs Brunning, Mrs Barker, Mrs Johnson.

PARADE OF SCHOOLCHILDREN in celebration of George V's coronation, Balderton, 6 May 1910. Pictured standing (left foreground) opposite Woodbine Terrace on London Road are Mrs Florence Bilton and her son, George. Wheeling her mother in the bath chair (centre, back) is Miss Louise Clark who delivered the post in the village.

MAIN STREET, BALDERTON, looking north. On the left is the Rose and Crown, a short way up from which stands John Bilton. Beneath the tree the churchwarden is deep in conversation with Mr Monty Wells, the local carrier, in his horse and trap.

CODDINGTON TOWER MILL dates from the eighteenth century. In the nineteenth century (1862) a small 10 hp steam engine was installed to allow working even on calm days. The mill remained operational until the Second World War when it fell into disrepair.

CODDINGTON NATIONAL SCHOOL. Erected in 1846 by public subscription and a grant from the National Society, the first master and mistress were Edward Unwin and his wife, Mary. The roll usually contained between sixty and seventy pupils, so this picture from c. 1900 is no doubt of the entire school.

PLANE CRASH, Coddington, 23 May 1939. The plane, a Handley Page Hampden of 7 Squadron RAF, crashed when control was lost while changing over pilots on a training flight. All five crew were killed and the plane was a write-off.

A PICTURESQUE VIEW of the entrance to Winthorpe. The distinctive red-brick church dates from 1886, being consecrated two years later in June 1888. The total cost was £4,000 which was borne by the Rector, Revd E. Handley. Two new bells were given by J.G. Branston of Winthorpe Grange.

WINTHORPE GRANGE, c. 1915. When this picture was taken the Grange was owned by Joseph Gilstrap Branston JP (1838–1926), a member of the prominent Branston malting family and nephew of Sir William Gilstrap. A Trent Navigation Commissioner for fifty years, Branston was also the instigator of many civic improvements in Newark.

WINTHORPE. Other than that it is thought to be Hargon House, Hargon Lane, Winthorpe in the 1890s, nothing more is known of this picture.

A FINAL VIEW of the picturesque lanes of Winthorpe.

FLOODS IN ROLLESTON, 1923. Pictured outside nos 9 and 10 Main Street are Mr and Mrs Parnham with their daughter (paddling).

HOLME CHURCH, showing one of the superbly carved oak pew ends. In addition to paired dogs with collars (seen here), other pews feature birds and angels, either side of large poppy-head mouldings.

'RED TIN COTTAGE', Main Street, Holme, c. 1910. Standing on the left is the owner, Mrs Robinson, while on the right is Miss Minnie Hartley.

MR J. HALLAM'S FARM, Holme, c. 1915. This picture shows one of his oldest workers, Mr Frederick John Cobb.

THE CHURCH OF ST WILFRID, North Muskham, parts of which date from c. 1190. The church was entirely restored in 1906, about the time this picture was taken. Unfortunately nothing is known of the lady cyclists.

NORTH MUSKHAM GRANGE, showing the main entrance façade. Although dating from the sixteenth century, it was greatly extended in the 1780s. In 1789 it was purchased by its most distinguished owner, William Rastall Dickinson, whose history of Southwell is still the principal work on the town. The Grange was demolished in the mid-1960s.

NORTH MUSKHAM BOARD SCHOOL, Class 1. The school was endowed in 1727 and 1745 by local benefactress Mary Woolhouse Disney, although the building used by these pupils was built in 1881. At the time this photograph was taken (1890s) the schoolmaster was Joseph Woodward.

CHILDREN FROM NORTH MUSKHAM SCHOOL in costume for one of their annual concerts of songs and sketches, c. 1931. They are, left to right: Jack Guy, Dick Jackson, Arthur Temprel, Paddy Mercheson and Sid Thurman. Unfortunately the title of the play is not known.

TRENT VILLAS, NORTH MUSKHAM. Visible behind the Misses Woods, Trent Villas was operated as a riverside café until the 1950s for day trippers from Newark. Some years ago it was damaged by fire and pulled down.

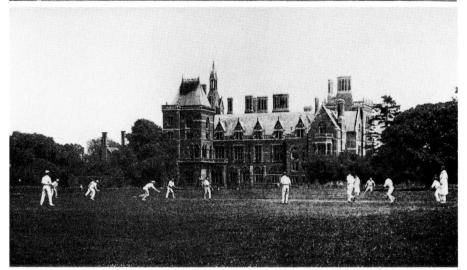

CRICKET AT KELHAM. The former Palladian house at Kelham burned down in 1857. John Manners-Sutton (MP for Newark) quickly engaged George Gilbert Scott to design a replacement. Scott, whose later work included St Pancras station (note the similarity), produced a masterpiece so expensive that it eventually led to the sale of the estate (1898) with the house still incomplete.

FOLLOWING THE 1898 SALE, Kelham Hall was taken over by the Society of the Sacred Mission (SSM) who set up their theological college there in 1903. Pictured here is a quiet corner of the SSM's library.

THE SSM EXTENDED KELHAM by building this remarkable domed chapel in the Arts and Crafts style in 1927–8. Standing atop a segmental brick arch, the great bronze rood (comprising a crucifix flanked by Mary and St John) was sculpted by Sargent Jagger.

BOTH GARAGE AND ADJACENT POST OFFICE at Kelham Corner were kept in the 1930s by Mr Jarvis Emmerson. Contributing to the eventual closure of the garage was its highly dangerous location on this once busy corner.

FARNDON FERRY, C. 1921, from the Rolleston and Staythorpe side of the Trent. In the background, right of the swing boats, lies the Britannia Inn (now 'The Lazy Otter'), while behind the flagpole is Bob Gravell's dance hall and tea room, built on stilts to avoid flooding.

OLIVE HOUSE, 16 Main Street, Farndon. In the 1890s this was the home of Matthew Herrod, willow grower, who supplied peeled willow to Horace Mills' basket manufactory on Farndon Road. Save for the removal of plum trees from the front garden, the house remains largely unaltered to this day.

THE OLD POST OFFICE, 16 West End, Farndon, 1898. Pictured are Lizzie Wilson with her daughter Elsie and stepson Freddie who lived opposite the post office. The post office closed in c. 1930 and is now a private residence known as 'The Cottage'.

FARNDON MILL was owned by Horace Stray, brother of Joseph Stray who kept the animal feed shop in Boar Lane, Newark. The mill ground corn and pigmeal for local farmers. In the mid-1920s Mr Stray emigrated to New Zealand and the mill fell into disrepair. Today only the brick tower remains, much dilapidated. Seen here left of the mill is Horace Mills' basket manufactory.

SUTTON-ON-TRENT. Purportedly a photograph of the first motor car in the village, c. 1900. Owned by Dr Arthur Naylor, it is pictured on what became the A1 through Sutton near the now defunct Crow Park railway station.

THE BRIDGE, Sutton-on-Trent.

SUTTON-ON-TRENT WINDMILL was built in 1825. A century later (in 1924) it had lost two of its four sails, although the Bingham family continued to use wind power until c. 1928. From that time until the Second World War (when milling ceased altogether) an oil engine was used. Coarse 'grist' corn was milled for cattle, while finer stones produced flour.

THE OLD VOLUNTEER, Sutton-on-Trent. Stephen Granger (pictured right) took over the pub from Mr Arthur Surgey in 1926–7, remaining landlord until c. 1930. Today the building has been converted to a private house.

Forshaws' Shire Horses

SEASON 1922.

KEEP THE LORRY IN VIEW.

PRINCE FORESTER

30806.

This horse has Government License for 1922.

Owners—JAS. FORSHAW & SONS,
CARLTON-ON-TRENT, Newark.

Telegrams   Station—
Sutton-on-Trent.   Carlton-on-Trent.

Whartons, Stud Printers, Retford.

TRADE CARD FROM JAMES FORSHAW & SONS, shire horse breeders of Sutton-on-Trent. Between 1886 and 1939 Forshaws became the largest such breeders in the country. Travelling by rail, their stallions sired progeny all over the country for a farming industry still largely dependent on the heavy horse for both operational and motive power.

AN EARLY AUTOMATIC REAPER in use at Toll Bar Farm, Car Colston, 1890s. Holding the horses is Charlie Pilkington (1891–1980). The following four pictures are all connected with the Pilkington family and their farming activities during the early part of this century.

HOLME INN FARM, SUTTON, which was taken over by the Pilkington family in 1902. Holme Inn itself was attached to the farm and, as well as working the farm, Charlie's father, Henry Pilkington, also acted as landlord.

SUTTON-ON-TRENT. Pictured at Holme Inn Farm in c. 1904–6 are Charlie Pilkington and brother, Tom, with their father, Henry Pilkington, holding the horse.

MEMBERS OF THE PILKINGTON FAMILY in the yard at Holme Inn Farm, c. 1904–6. They are, left to right: Henry Pilkington, Charlie Pilkington (on horse), Ethel Pilkington and Flossie Pilkington (sisters of Charlie). The figure on the far right is unknown.

STEAM THRESHING at Holme Inn Farm, Sutton-on-Trent, c. 1904–6. In adult life, Charlie Pilkington (seen here on the horse left) became a thresher and continued in this line until retirement in 1955. Before his death in 1980 he passed on his threshing skills to staff at the Museum of Lincolnshire Life, Lincoln, where traction engines, local threshing machinery, and a bust of Charlie are on display.

FISKERTON WATER MILL. Built in the eighteenth century as a lace thread factory, it was converted to a corn mill in 1837. When this picture was taken (c. 1901) the mill was owned by William Marriott (astride motorbike), while the manager was Leonard Longden (standing in doorway). The mill was operational as recently as 1987.

VIRTUALLY THE ENTIRE VILLAGE gathered at Flintham Hall for this group photograph in celebration of Queen Victoria's Golden Jubilee, 1887. The Hall, ancestral home of the Thoroton-Hildyards, was then let to a Mr Edward Elsey, a bookmaker from Nottingham. 103 years later, on 17 November 1990, this scene was re-enacted by photographer Trevor Clayton and the present residents of Flintham.

FLINTHAM HALL is essentially a Georgian building (although claiming medieval origins), on to which, in the 1850s, the Nottingham architect T.C. Hine grafted a series of exuberant Italianate façades. Most prominent among Hine's alterations is the magnificent conservatory (right) which remains, without doubt, the finest surviving Victorian conservatory in England.

FLINTHAM MAIN STREET, C. 1900. The van (left) is thought to be either that of the village baker, W.R. Rylatt, or of one of the two local carriers, C. Thurman (to Nottingham) or W. Perkins (to Newark). Far right is the village shop, 'The Stores', kept between 1910 and 1982 by the White family.

FREDERICK ARTHUR WHITE was the proprietor of the village shop between 1910 and 1949. He began his working life as a draper in Chesterfield before moving to Flintham to take over 'The Stores'. Mr White was a keen amateur photographer and the remaining shots of Flintham are all taken from his original glass negatives. It is not known why Mr White photographed himself here in uniform.

THE WHITE FAMILY HOME, Flintham. Upon arrival at Flintham in 1910 Mr White set up home in the cottage on the corner of Main Street and Woods Lane. Pictured here are his wife, Mary Elizabeth (Lizzie), and daughter, Muriel May, aged 3–4 (with teddy bear). Still largely unchanged today, the property is now known as Old Barn Cottage.

WILLIAM GELL, removal contractor and coal merchant, of Kneeton Road, East Bridgford, is pictured in Woods Lane during one of his deliveries to Flintham. In the distance stands the now demolished Primitive Methodist chapel.

BADGER BAITING, Flintham Woods on the Flintham Hall estate, pre-1914. Considered verminous and harmful to cattle, badgers were hunted using a live specimen (on leash) to flush out the others from the set. If necessary a spade was used to reach the entrenched animals.

SLATED ROW, FLINTHAM. Now known as High Bank, these cottages on Main Street were given their original name because they had roofs of slate rather than the locally predominant pantile.

HAY-MAKING at Grange Farm, Flintham in September 1914. This is purportedly the last photograph taken by Frederick White. Immediately after taking this shot Mr White's camera is said to have been blown over by a gust of wind and irreparably damaged. From that day forth he never took another photograph.

H.R.H. The Prince of Wales shaking hands with W. Jacklin, The Rufford Huntsman, at a Meet at Winkburn Hall Jan 10th 1928.

HOWARD BARRETT SOUT

THE HALL AT WINKBURN dates back to William and Mary although considerable additions were made in the 1840s. The home of the Burnell family for nine generations, in 1928 it was the residence of Major Edward Annesley Pegge Burnell-Smith-Milnes.

ELSTON HALL, home of the noted poet and botanist, Erasmus Darwin FRS (1731–1802). Erasmus was the grandfather of Charles Darwin who, in 1859, published the revolutionary *Origin of Species*. Charles' branch of the family, however, never lived at Elston, but at Downe in Kent.

THE OLD HORSE AND GEARS PUBLIC HOUSE, Elston, now Corner Cottage and Hollydene. On the far left is the pub's brewhouse (now demolished), while in the distance are the Bridge Cottages.

THE VILLAGE GROCERY SHOP AND POST OFFICE, Elston, 1922. Shopkeeper and postmistress was Miss Emily Beeston. Her housekeeper, Miss Moriss (pictured here) delivered telegrams.

HALL FARM COTTAGES (now the post office), Elston. The lady in the bonnet is believed to be Mrs Blatherwick, while to the left (with apron) is Mrs Brambley with the daughters of Mr William Merrin, owner of Hall Farm.

MERRIN'S FARM, Elston, pre-1914. The threshing machine is belt-driven from the steam traction engine. Merrin's stackyard with lime trees is visible in the background.

HALL FARM with the Merrin family, Elston.

JASMINE COTTAGES WITH DOVE COTTAGE in the background, Elston, c. 1907. Standing before the cottages are, left to right: Mrs Brawley, Miss Lucy Long, Mrs Long, Mrs Brawley (sister-in-law to the first Mrs Brawley) and Mrs Martin with her children, Winnie and Leslie. The identity of the three children in the foreground is not known.

THE 'BLACK GIANT' OF ELSTON. Built in 1844, Elston Mill passed to the Gash family in 1919. Here, and at another mill in Long Bennington, they produced foodstuffs for farm animals. In the 1920s, however, Elston Mill became the original base of William Gash's 'bus service.

THE FIRST PURPOSE-BUILT MOTOR 'BUS obtained by Gash was this 1926 Reo Sprinter. Costing £628 and painted blue and cream it remained in service for ten years. A roofrack was provided for the carriage of general goods and small items of livestock such as chickens.

A LEYLAND TITAN 'BUS, built in 1931, but not acquired by Gash until July 1947. It stayed with them for exactly three years before being withdrawn in July 1950. Pictured are driver Fred Morley and 'clippy' Betty Tart.

THE FORGE, LOW STREET, Elston, 1920s. The blacksmith Mr Frederick Mann RSS (Registered Shoeing Smith) is pictured centre (with hands on hips). Behind him is Mr Beeston, while next right is Mr Clark, blacksmith's assistant. Mrs Clark stands on the far left behind the gate. Note the farm implements awaiting repair on the far right behind George Greensmith.

ELSTON TOWERS was built in 1872–5 for Robert Middleton, 'a religious zealot of the Baptist persuasion'. Photographs of country house construction are rare, but here Middleton's entire workforce are recorded for posterity. Far left is Edwin Hunter (1844–1919) the builder, while far right is his father, Joseph Hunter (1818–99). The only other known person in the picture is 'The Boy Scarboro' sitting in the centre.

MIDDLETON'S CLOCK TOWER (now demolished) is of particular note at Elston Towers. Instead of chiming the hours, the bells possessed a repertoire of twenty-eight tunes including hymns and such popular Victorian melodies as *Home Sweet Home, The Blue Bells of Scotland* and *There's no Luck about the House on a Washing Day*. The house quickly became known as 'Middleton's Folly'.

ELSTON TOWERS, by contemporary standards, cost an enormous amount to build – over £30,000. Middleton, however, did not forsake his Baptist roots: the main entrance to the house led straight into a private chapel, seen here some years after Middleton's death when it was the home of Joseph Truman, a lace manufacturer. Still largely intact today, the building survives as the Coeur de Lion restaurant.

ELSTON SCHOOL INFANTS' CLASS, 1924. Back row, left to right: Miss Kingston (teacher), Charlie Slater, Bill Greensmith, Albert Bond, George Huskinson, Francis Sterling, Fred Bond, Revd Howard (Rector). Middle row: Mona Doncaster, Jessie Marlin, Joan Blatherwick, Pauline Flatman, Alma Hallam, Winnie Slater, Bessie Hopkinson, Monica Blatherwick, Mary Spinks, Roy Hopkinson. On chairs: Margaret Hully, Eva Simms, Leslie Bailey.

The Hall, East Stoke

EAST STOKE HALL. Sanctioned in 1332 as a hospital for the poor, the present building dates from c. 1800 and was once home of the Bromley family of bankers. The best known member of the family was Lord Pauncefote who was the first British Ambassador to the United States.

MAIN STREET, EAST STOKE, at around the turn of the century. This pot-holed track now forms the A46 (Fosse Way). On the right stands the Pauncefote Arms. The cottages on the left have since been demolished.

MAIN STREET, EAST STOKE, c. 1900.

CAUNTON MANOR with Major Hugh Hole. The Manor was formerly the home of Samuel Reynolds Hole (1819–1904), Dean of Rochester and a noted rose grower. In 1858 he instigated the first National Rose Show and was the first President of the Rose Society from 1876 until his death.

THE HOLE ARMS, Caunton. The building dates back around 400 years, during which time it has also been known as 'The Harrow' and 'The Manor Arms'. It is now no longer a public house and is currently awaiting conversion to private dwellings.

MISS JINNY TAYLOR of the Grange, Caunton
– a noted local artist and well-known
figure in the village.

MISS CHARLOTTE GILBERT, housekeeper to the Misses Taylor at Caunton Grange, c. 1890s.

HAY-MAKING at Woovers Farm, Caunton, mid-1920s. Left to right: Mr Woods, Mr Charles Taylor (owner, on top of cart) and Tom Duffin.

AN EARLY PETROL-DRIVEN TRACTOR photographed on an unknown farm in Caunton. Pictured are Ernest Lambert and Harry Gilbert.

FLOODING OFF MAIN STREET, Caunton, 1922. On the left is the Hole Arms, while behind the central group is the village shop and post office.

CAUNTON CHURCH OF ENGLAND SCHOOL was built in 1840 with the aim of educating the poor children of the parish. As in most country areas, however, school work often took second place to such necessities as harvesting, potato picking, bird scaring and willow rod peeling. This school group dates from the 1890s.

ANNE ELVIDGE was one of the oldest residents in Caunton when photographed. She died not long after this picture was taken in c. 1896.

'BIRDSEYE' VIEW from the church of St John the Baptist, South Collingham, looking north-east. On the far left is Westfield Lane passing before Burnt House and Stocks Hill. This postcard was post-marked December 1906.

BREWSTER'S GARAGE, Collingham, in the 1950s. To the left stands the Crown Inn, while on the right is Thompson's butchers. Note the position of Brewster's petrol pumps right up against the fourteenth-century village cross. The cross was finally removed to the Green in 1970. The garage is now owned by the Durham brothers.

A BUSY SCENE AT COLLINGHAM WHARF, Trent Lane, around the turn of the century featuring the *Robin Hood* paddle steam tug.

PIG ON THE LINE! The crossing house at Cottage Lane, Collingham, on the Midland Railway's Nottingham–Lincoln line, c. 1895. The crossing house was demolished in 1914.

CARROTS ARRIVING AT COLLINGHAM STATION. Collingham was once known for its carrots which grew well in the sandy soil. There were four carrot washers in the station yard, three powered by gas and one by oil. In the picture are, left to right: Carlo the dog, David Nicholson, Joe Witt, Charles Liley, Jack Harris and Henry Liley holding the horse.

WASHED AND BAGGED CARROTS were loaded at Collingham station each evening to ensure their arrival at market in Manchester by 6 a.m. Here, loading the bags, are, left to right: Jane Liley, Henry Liley, Doris Liley, Elsie Liley and Len Hawkins. Supervising is Collingham station master Arthur Kind.

BARTHOLEMEW 'THOL' WAITE, blacksmith, making a Collingham 'sprittle' – a kind of push hoe with changeable blades for hoeing different vegetables. Thol had his smithy in Challands Yard, later moving to 'The Forge' opposite the Grey Horse public house. He died in 1959, aged 78.

WILLIAM PRIDMORE, saddler, harness-maker and shoe-repairer, Collingham. Mr Pridmore had his shop at the corner of High Street and Swinderby Road (now North House) until his death in 1969. Pictured in the trap is Joe Cook.

GEORGE MOSS, plough maker, wheelwright and undertaker outside his High Street workshop, North Collingham, c. 1906. A plough maker of national renown, Moss' 'Gem' plough boasted 'over 50 all England prizes ... prov[ing] itself to be the plough of the day' (advertisement). Moss' business faded in the 1920s, and the re-built shed (right) is now occupied by 'The Barn' fruit and vegetable shop.

FLOODS IN LOW STREET, Collingham, 26 May 1932. Riding the tide are Mr Moseley and his daughter.

POTATO PICKERS, Collingham. Left to right: David Nicholson, Hilda Moore, Lily Moore, Len Liley and Alice Collingham.

WILLIAM BAILEY, baker and flour merchant of 15 High Street, North Collingham, c. 1890. Although the bakery business declined in the mid-1950s, the Bailey family still occupy the same premises today, trading as Agricultural Merchants. In memory of their former business, the building has been re-named 'The Old Bakehouse'.

STAFF AT HEALEY'S GARAGE, High Street, South Collingham, summer 1923. Right to left: Ernest Healey (founder and proprietor), George Osborne (mechanic), Raymond Newstead (mechanic), and Harold Healey (son of proprietor). They are leaning against a 1920 Rover, property of Joseph Gibson, farmer. The business remained in the Healey family until 1971 when Harold Healey retired.

HEALEY'S GARAGE WAS THE BIRTHPLACE of a most remarkable vehicle in the late 1960s. The 'Double Mini' was designed by Malcolm Skeel (left) as an engineering stunt. Even so it was fully operational at both ends and licensed for use on the road . . . And you couldn't see the join! Also pictured are coachbuilder Frank Jessop and Harold Healey (centre), garage owner.

COLLINGHAM FIRE BRIGADE, c. 1918. Believed to be a stand at Collingham Show, the four firemen seen here are, left to right: William Thompson, Alfred Wiseman, William Wiseman and Albert Holland.

DECORATIONS FOR THE CORONATION of Edward VII, North Collingham, 1902. The left hand house was the home of Henry Skerrit, that on the right belonging to Fred Skerrit. Later, these premises housed Mr Pankhurst's cobblers shop, Mrs Woodend's sweet shop and Mr Morrell's photographic studio.

GEORGINA DENISON and friend Christopher Prestwich before Ossington Hall, January 1963. The central portion of the Hall dates from c. 1728 and is attributed to James Gibbs. The Denisons came to Ossington in 1768 when William Denison, a wealthy Leeds woollen-cloth exporter bought the estate from the Cartwright family. The hall was demolished in 1963, although the Denisons continued to reside on the estate at nearby Ossington House.

OSSINGTON HALL FROM THE TERRACE. When William Denison bought the estate in 1768 it was run-down, producing only a very low income. Fired with the same energy that had proved so successful in the woollen trade, Denison resolved to improve it. By the time he died in 1782 the estate was one of the most productive in Nottinghamshire.

MISS GEORGINA DENISON, daughter of Lt-Col William Maxwell Evelyn Denison, feeding her hand-reared pheasants in the park at Ossington Hall, September 1957.

(P. Goedhuis)

ACKNOWLEDGEMENTS

I wish to express my sincere thanks to the following without whom the production of this book would not have been possible. To Miss J.M. Antoine for permission to reproduce photographs from original negatives taken by her father, Mr N.J. Antoine, in the 1930s and '40s. To Roy Wells, 'King Bygone', for access to his extensive collection of photographs and postcards which, together with those of Miss Antoine, form the backbone of this compilation. Thereafter to Mr R.A.J. Vinnicombe, Newark District Librarian, and Sheila M. Cooke and Dorothy Ritchie of the Nottingham Local Studies Library for advice, support and encouragement.

The numerous individuals and organizations who have loaned photographs for use in this collection are listed below together with page references.

Miss J.M. Antoine: 9, 10a, 13a, 15a, 15b, 17a, 17b, 23b, 34a, 41a, 49, 50a, 50b, 52a, 54a, 57a, 58a, 63b, 65a, 74a, 76a, 78b, 80a, 80b, 82b, 83b, 87b, 88a, 88b, 90b, 92b, 93a, 93b, 94a, 95b, 97a, 98a, 98b, 99a, 99b, 100a, 100b, 101a, 101b, 102, 110. Mr W. Bailey: 73b. Mr R. Baker: 114b. Balderton Parish Council: 104a. Mrs B.W. Barker: 117a, 117b, 118. Mrs E.M. Beckett: 125b, 126a, 126b, 127a, 127b. Mr D.E. Bilton: 105a, 105b, 107a, 107b, 108. British Gypsum Ltd: 32b, 33a, 33b. Caunton Local History Society: 145a, 145b, 146a, 146b, 147a, 147b, 148a, 148b, 149. Mrs E.M. Clark: 47a, 77. Collingham Museum Committee: 150b, 151a, 151b, 152a, 152b, 153a, 153b, 154a, 154b, 155a, 155b, 156a, 157a, 157b. Mr S. Dimmock: 140b, 141a, 141b. Mrs J.M. Edge: 106b. Mr A.R. Edwards: 59a. Mrs P. Goedhuis: 158a, 159. Miss M. Granger: 116b, 124a, 124b, 158b. Mrs M. Hackney: 122a. Mr H. Hall: 44a, 44b, 45a, 45b, 73a, 96a. Mr H.J. Healey: 156b. Mrs W.H. Hopewell: 19a, 53b, 62a. Mrs M. Hopkinson: 78a. Mrs E.M. Kemp: 47b, 113. Lilley & Stone Upper School: 21a, 23a. Mr H.J. Mackender: 84a, 84b. Newark and Sherwood College: 16a, 16b, 55b. Newark Salvation Army: 57b, 65b, 89a. Mrs E.M. O'Connell: 69a, 74b. Mr G. Peabody: 135a, 135b, 136a, 136b, 137a, 137b, 138a, 138b, 139a, 139b, 140a, 142. Mr E. Pinkney: 30a, 40a, 40b, 58b, 66b. Mrs N. Postles: 60a, 61a. Mrs E. Potts: 20a, 20b, 36a. Mrs M. Richmond: 79a, 79b. Mr B. Robb: 87a. Mr J.V. Robinson: 37a, 37b. Mr J. Rodgers: 51a. Mr F.M. Rouse: 10b, 11a, 11b, 18b, 29a, 54b, 59b. Dr J. Samuels: 128. Miss G.A. Shipman: 106a. Mr P. Speirs: 72a, 72b. Mrs E.M. Stray: 122b. Thomas Magnus Upper School: 24b, 25a, 25b, 26a, 26b, 27a, 27b, 28a. Mr G.R. Tindale: 129a. Mr H. Turner: 39b, 53a. Mr R. Wells: 12b, 14b, 18a, 19b, 22a, 28b, 29b, 30b, 31, 32a, 34b, 35b, 36b, 38a, 41b, 42a, 42b, 43a, 43b, 48a, 48b, 52b, 56a, 56b, 60b, 62b, 64a, 64b, 67a, 68a, 68b, 69b, 70a, 71, 76b, 82a, 83a, 86b, 90a, 91a, 92a, 96b, 97b, 111a, 111b, 112a, 112b, 114a, 115, 116a, 119b, 120a, 120b, 121a, 121b, 123a, 125a, 130a, 134, 143a, 143b, 150a. Mrs E. Welthorpe: 22b, 75a, 75b, 109a. Miss E.A. Whistler: 14a. Mr B. White (for J.L. Maltby & Sons): 46a, 46b, 63a. Miss G.M. White: 81a, 81b. Miss M.M. White: 130b, 131a, 131b, 132a, 132b, 133. Mr P. Whiteley (for Charles Street Methodist Church): 66a, 89b. Mr T. Wright (for Wright & Sons Coach Hire): 38b, 39a.